FINAL CUT

Saleem Peeradina was born in Mumbai, India in 1944. He is the author of four previous collections of poetry, and a prose memoir of growing up in Bombay, *The Ocean in My Yard* (Penguin, 2005). He was editor of *Contemporary Indian Poetry in English* (Macmillan, 1972), one of the earliest and most widely used texts in courses on South Asian literature. He currently lives in Michigan, and is Emeritus Professor of English at Siena Heights University.

Final Cut

SALEEM PEERADINA

Valley Press

First published in 2016 by Valley Press
Woodend, The Crescent, Scarborough, UK, YO11 2PW
www.valleypressuk.com

ISBN 978-1-908853-68-4
Cat. no. VP0085

A CIP record for this book is available from the British Library.

Contents

A Note of Thanks

For those friends who told me their stories.

For those unexpected gifts that introduced me to new backyard visitors.

For those simple objects I saved and cherished that spoke to me.

For the cultivators of fruits that arrived all the way into my kitchen.

For those devoted writers and dedicated researchers who enlightened my mind with their revelations, and whose insights proved priceless.

And my ardent readers and listeners who rewarded me with their attention.

And for Cindy Anderson, the Humanities Office manager, a bouquet of thanks – for her infinite patience, and her always-cheerful readiness to get the poems typed and into the proper electronic format.

Acknowledgments

A few poems in this book have been previously published by coldnoon.com, *Eclipse*, *Muse-India*, *Peninsula Poets*, undergroundflowers.com and *World Literature Today*.

Many of the 'bird' poems in this book are found poems, based on *Birds of Michigan* by Ted Black and Gregory Kennedy.

The 'fruit' poems in this book are based on a combination of observation, recollection of memories associated with the fruits, the history of their origins, and the experience and rituals of eating them. For the factual details, I have had to rely on information available on Wikipedia.

Author's Note

Strictly speaking, for the poet who exercises his/her art exclusively in the service of writing poetry, deliberate thought is rarely given to explaining the factors surrounding its composition. The poetry alone is enough and should speak for itself. Everything else is redundant.

On the other hand, poets who work in related disciplines or multiple areas often give conscious thought to the process that separates or integrates the two or more practices. Teaching is one of those occupations that forces one to examine all the implications endemic to the craft of writing. Especially when it comes to the teaching of writing, these questions are unavoidable and indeed ought to be raised. The useful part for students, lay readers, reviewers, scholars, is to view poetry in its totality: above all, the poet's handling of language, structure, tone, and meaningful statement. In addition, an awareness of process from start to finish, the cultural context from which it springs, the transnational geographies in which it is rooted, its ideological underpinnings, and the seriousness with which the writer's intent is communicated. This can not only promote the reader's comprehension and enjoyment, but also help determine the poem's quality and worth.

Thus, it is the educator in me who wants to raise these questions. Hence, this note about the genesis of this book.

Animals have wandered into my poems in earlier books, but not in the extended way of the birds that have migrated into this book. There is ample precedent in literature of poets who write about animals and offer deep insights and beauty. To name only a few – Blake, Keats, Shelly, D.H. Lawrence, Marianne Moore, and Ted Hughes have all left a record of memorable poetry in this genre. I am fascinated as well by studies of animal intelligence, communication, and inter-species love: not only between animals and humans, but also between species traditionally thought to be hostile to one another in the food chain.

I am indebted, more than in any other book of mine, to scholars and researchers who devote their lives to exploring subjects and ideas that further our understanding of the world. My taste in reading stretches far beyond the realm of literature, because I have an inexhaustible curiosity for discovering new worlds both interior and external. For medical issues, two of my favorite authors are Oliver Sacks and Atul Gawande. Gawande in fact, in addition to his surgical expertise, insight, and compassion, is a fine prose stylist, better than many writers of fiction and non-fiction. I am also fascinated by the writings of E.O. Wilson, whose *The Naturalist* tells his own story of how he developed an interest in ants and other insects and where it led him.

Learning about the spice trade, the histories of salt, pepper, tea, sugar, cotton and slave-trafficking, revealed the brutal and bloody politics of imperial expansion. A book about fruits, with close-ups and short descriptions, opened a whole new dimension which I had been part of on a daily basis since childhood, but to which I never gave much conscious thought.

A couple of poems from my friend Adil Jussawala's fine 2011 book, *Trying to Say Goodbye*, started me on the 'object' poems. It was truly thrilling to realize that objects I had been using or storing could be nudged to narrate their own stories. Two of these objects belonged to other people.

Sometimes, reading does not result immediately in an outcome in poetry. A book like Jennifer Hecht's *Doubt,* a wide-ranging and carefully researched history of skepticism, has to circulate in one's arteries before one can assimilate it into a personal world view. Another hard-to-classify contemporary writer, Alain de Botton, had me hooked on *The Consolations of Philosophy*, and since then, I have read every non-fiction book of his on subjects ranging from travel to architecture. Then, along with other influences from fields as diverse as cosmology, evolution, genetics, anthropology and philosophy, poems such as 'The Lesson', 'Close Call' and 'The View from Seventy' could surface.

If I had to borrow a term from cultural anthropology, I would say that for me, the act of writing poetry is like being a participant-observer who is engaged in doing ethnography. Nothing is out of bounds.

Saleem Peeradina
May 2015

The Lesson

Take a sheet of paper the size of a drawing pad. The universe,
as we perceive it, must be accommodated within the borders
of this rectangle. Draw a circle the size of a marble to represent
the Earth, then hitch the moon to it. This travel companion will never
leave the Earth's side. Now surround them with planets in their proper

elliptical positions. Reserve a central place for the sun. Cram the entire
backdrop with stars, thumbing in a smudge to mark the Milky Way.
Then set the whole facsimile in motion, in perpetual
rotations and revolutions.

But you are not done yet. Fold this sheet
to fashion an origami pigeon and release this messenger bird
into the sky. It will quickly reach a vanishing point flying among
billions of other winged creatures, each carrying its own universe.

If your head is spinning, try this: crumple the piece of paper
and store it in the black hole of your pocket never to be found again
by anyone.

There is a third alternative. Place this sheet at one end
of a panoramic screen and proceed to jump off the brink of our universe
into neighboring galaxies spiraling outward, endlessly. Shrunk, relegated
to a corner, our universe is virtually erased, leaving us adrift.
Here, far beyond imagination's reach, infinity unravels leaving us
speechless. But seeking solace in myths will get us nowhere.

We have to make the journey back to reclaim the Earth. As we start to
descend and fall towards what seems like a speck of dust, it turns into a rock;
then, this enormous circular globe packed with mountains, oceans, forests, all
suspended, frozen at two ends and burning elsewhere, this jewel
of an Earth, this blue planet escorted by clouds, which has hauled its rich
load of life for millions of years, not straying from its given path,
but gliding, floating, owning this alien but familiar space, returns

to our side, smooth, unruffled, like the messenger bird back from its epic
pilgrimage, finding the ball of crumpled paper saved in our pocket.

You, in a Dream

It was a day like any other
on a street cut for small town living: church steeple,
shops with apartments above, cafes, a medley
font of store signs, yawning idlers, distracted
children and suddenly – you – waiting
as you always did, under an awning
against red brick lit up by sunlight and shade,
your lips shaping a silent smile
in the very next instant, dissolving, fading…

Slipping forward out of history's past, I was
Zhivago on a tram and you, Lara, so near,
on the pavement heading out of view
to a future I could not hold back
with a wave or a shout. If I missed you
by a heartbeat, I missed you by a century.

Embedded

Based on an art work by Pallavi Sharma

It is my sky, my earth, the four corners of my world.
My valley, my meadow, from end to end, my entire
ocean floor. When I stretched my hand, I was given
five fruits. Just plucked. The strawberries glowed
against the grain of my knuckles, my skin showing signs
of wear beside the taut fruit plump with blood.
These hands have caressed, guided, comforted, but

these fingers are strangers to dirt. I have not earned
these jewels gifted by those whose limbs have sweated
in the fields. The taste of one I bit into – so lush, so cool –
will linger all season long. The remainder, their freshness
tinged with the morning dew, I will preserve like museum
exhibits embedded in the rich tapestry of my nightly dreams.

The Daughter's Lament

It has been hectic since you left.
Mom fell sick. Again. I am losing count.
She cannot do the four storeys down and up
anymore. I had to take the day off
to have the doctor visit her, the nurse to do
all the tests, and the physiotherapist who sees her
at home. As you know, her vision is not so good
but at least she can feel her way around the house
when I am at work.

On that front, the midnight shift
is punishing. It is hard to get enough sleep during
the day what with the noise all around.

Water problems continue. And they will get worse
until the monsoon arrives. The ceiling has developed
cracks and pieces of concrete keep falling.
The society says it is my responsibility to get it
repaired. I am looking around for a contractor
I can trust and since the relatives are reluctant to help
financially, I will have to apply for a bank loan.
Two hundred and fifty thousand rupees is no joke.

As you know, Dad didn't leave much when he died
five years ago. I am the sole earner now. And how will
I get time off from work to supervise the repairs?
You know we can't leave it up to the contractor
to comply with the agreement in a timely fashion
whether it is verbal or written down.

As if that was not enough, my computer conked off.
It is a good thing I have the phone as a back-up
which you so kindly helped me to buy before you left.

Meanwhile, my relatives keep bringing proposals
from suitors, a few of whom I have met. But as soon as
they hear about my sick mother being part of
the package, they lose interest. I don't blame them.

Anyway, who is to say getting hitched will solve the problem
or make it worse? Even though I am past my mid-thirties,
I have the example of my younger sister whose
marriage is a mess. From time to time, I have her
and her two kids who come and stay with me as she goes
back and forth to her in-laws pretty much with no resolution

in sight. Hers is the classic case of the husband caught between
the wife and his own family. What all this adds up to is that
I have to stand on my own and I have to get my priorities straight.

The View from Seventy

They're early settlers, entering the bloodstream bearing
gifts from their twin lineages. They lie dormant, waiting
to be guided by instinct to release their malignant
power. We are a stage, a squat; this is what we provide

from within: fertile soil for them to practice
their hit-and-run arts with the ease of those born
to be warriors. They come with clear intent – to occupy
what they claim as their ancestral stake – and they're here to stay.

Outside, all around, as indispensable as air and water, are others
slipping through the cracks. Our bodies are host to their
breeding but we are given the means to keep them in line.
We can go underground to join the Resistance. The enemy

to watch out for is the one who enters stealthily with unmarked
baggage. Like the seducer who played for years on the swings,
slides, and see-saw of my heart and eventually left me breathless.
The interloper has since relaxed his grip to become a permanent

member of the house, a seventh sense, sending occasional signals
of pain. Even with the *No Vacancy* sign, there will be intruders lurking
around who will try to force their way in. Some lodgers match
camouflage with decorum so well, we forget they are there.

We could fear these hangers on, but they make better companions
once we befriend them. They belong to us as much as our
other faculties of smell, taste, or touch. We can uncover
their secrets, test their limits, learn to use their guerilla tactics

against them. We know they are armed and dangerous.
And against their weaponry, we have no defense. Whether their siege
is short-lived or long, in the end, there is only one certainty:
true to their calling, they are obliged to take us down.

Close Call

It pays no attention to rules, nor does it follow
any creed. Random, relentless, unsparing, it defeats
those looking for the logic of its actions.
It can never be even-handed, so calling it perverse
is pointless. It has no need to be contrite.
Eyes closed, it operates with complete disinterest
in outcomes. Lacking motive, it is free of judgment.
It has a capricious sense of humor.

It wipes out entire populations with the sweep
of a broom. It haunts battlefields, epidemics,
natural disasters. An eruption registers on the Richter
scale – an island is swallowed up. In a final burst
of light, a star is snuffed out. Seasoned runners
entering the last lap never make it to the finish line.
It stalks the neighborhood to strike the house next door,
or shuffling up the stairs, it stomps the floor above.

When it appears to have laid aside its club, it
boomerangs to knock down your best friend, missing you
by a hair. Entire teams of relatives go down like
wickets falling. It makes light work of worldly honors.
The loss of family elders lies within the realm
of expectations. The passing of peers leaves you
exposed to the searchlight in the tower, sweeping
the ground for escapees. Dodging the beam

or hiding in the dark is not a choice that will save you.
Death was born to steal the show.

To an Old Friend

Last night, I thought I heard the rustle of a page
turning, a chapter closing. In the morning, when I went
to wake up my mother as I usually did every day,
I found her in a state of serene sleep. The last words
we exchanged when she went to bed were *good night*.

That was four months ago when I started writing this note
to you. It has taken me all this time to compose myself.
I still miss her deeply. She was ninety-one years old, and except for
a poor memory for names, she was in good shape and had led
a full life. She died in the best circumstance possible – in her own

bed – passing from one sleep into another. For the last two years
I was without any domestic help, since servants are so hard to find.
So, in addition to taking care of mother, I did all the cooking
and housework, with the result that I had little time for myself.
Going on seventy, I have my share of aches and pains.

Washing dishes and clothes I don't mind, but sweeping and
mopping the floors and cleaning the bathroom proves
difficult. With me slowing down too, you can see how full
my days are. My husband, who is a bit older, has developed
swollen feet and knees as a result of low hemoglobin count.

He refuses to have knee replacement surgery, but keeps
himself mobile for day-to-day activities with yogic exercises.
Since he cannot walk long distances, we go nowhere
and have become stay-at-home people. Only the fireplace,
an open book, and a dog curled up at his feet are missing.

Lest you think my life is an unrelieved saga of domestic drudgery
and health concerns, I have been blessed with six grand-children
ranging in age from seven to seventeen. They visit at different times
and bring a lot of joy and a bit of chaos to the household. I am also glad
to see my three children settled and thriving in their chosen fields.

Please do give me all the news from your end. I think our last contact
was more than a year ago but I think of you frequently and hope to
communicate more often. Until then, much affection.

A Rumor of Birds

After reading Songbird Journeys *by Miyoko Chu, 2006*

In my sleep, birds stream silently overhead – flocks of them –
wave after wave of a high altitude river unbound
by banks, wings riding the wind, navigating by stars in the pitch
black of night, or the water's magnetic glaze.
Sometimes, they storm above my roof in a cloudburst
of feathers, squawks, and screams.

One watching through a telescope will see them
scatter like flakes of pepper against lunar light.
but mostly, these night-travelers will pass invisibly, afloat
on a murmur. Before daybreak, they sift down
to settle in the trees or fields to awaken us with their
morning songs. After dusk, they flutter up again to migrate south.

Jays, thrushes, blackbirds, finches, wrens, larks, swallows, tanagers,
warblers, orioles – you live, love, breed, and die at full tilt
claiming only a bit of earth and infinite sky.

A Conference of Crows

It is nature's charcoal sketch of a bird.
Although it sports no colorful plumage,
has a raucous cry, dines on garbage, and makes
a picnic out of a roadside carcass, the bold,
intelligent, clever crow is worthy of great respect
for having flourished despite human efforts

to decimate its numbers. Like the house sparrow,
the common crow is everywhere – along coastlines,
on mountain tops, in deserts, and even the arctic regions.
Possessing an uncanny talent to adapt to any habitat,
the reputation it has earned is decidedly mixed:
glorified as a trickster in one place, the all-black raven

is feared elsewhere as a bird of ill-omen. If a crow caws
insistently on your window sill or balcony, you can prepare
for the arrival of a guest. For the mockers of superstitions
it is just a spoiler of sleep. Like the parrot, the crow
is an impressive mimic able to whine like a dog, squawk
like a hen, or cry like a baby. It shows its playful side

sliding down a slippery surface or harassing a flock
of gulls. It struts like a klutz fancying it can waltz.
Like a monkey, it watches for an opportune moment
to steal scraps from campers. Crows gather
in the hundreds to hold noisy rallies. A congregation
raises a parliamentary din, now recognized as

a murder of crows. Yet, this pragmatic, even
opportunistic bird has an almost sacred personal ethic:
crows maintain loyal, lifelong pair bonds, enduring
food scarcity and harsh weather to raise the young.
They live in close domestic proximity to us, but wary
of human intentions, they will not befriend us.

Because their ties with us are ageless, they let us
eavesdrop on their conference, so we may learn
to heed the call of the crow.

Blue Heron, in Three Frames

Found near freshwater and saltwater habitats,
the heron sports a blue-gray coat with a tinge of yellow
on its elongated neck. Its angular body strikes a ballerina's
pose but its real talent is standing motionless for hours, looking
blank, detached, like a Yogi. The black stripes over the eyes

on both sides of its head make no crown like the peacock's.
More like a headband with a quill sticking out. On its chest
is a cluster of quills fastidiously preened and kept clean.
The heron has a sleek figure, sinuous S-shaped neck which can
stretch and swivel at will, and reedy legs with three-pronged feet.

But that would not make it a comic bird. That distinction
belongs to the ostrich with its towering neck, startled eyes,
and stilt legs driving its tub of a body across the plains
like a chariot. The heron is nothing less than majestic in its
stately poise. When it breaks the silence, the sound

issuing from its throat is a squawk, a harsh croak, or a blast of
trumpet. It goes vocal in the breeding season, bill snapping
and chattering being quite common between paired
herons. They are known to be monogamous – for a
season – but tend to choose new partners each year.

*

As if waking from a trance, when this Stoic philosopher stirs,
it turns into a stalker. Fish is really at the top of its menu
but it can just as well make a meal out of insects, worms,
frogs, crabs, reptiles, mice, even smaller birds. With deliberate
steps it wades knee-deep in marsh water, neck drawn in,

and pretends to be a statue patiently scanning the surface
in a crouch position. When it spots a fish, the rubber neck darts
like a cobra's head making of its hard beak a spear to stab
its prey. In a flash it gulps down the fish in a single morsel.
Occasionally, when it is choking, it must cough it out.

*

Ready to launch from its perch, it starts out clumsy, taking a dive
upward. But soon this lumbering leap turns spectacular.
Unlike a swan that takes off at an angle, as if from
a watery runway, the heron rises in place in a vertical flutter.
It is the way storks and cranes, egrets, and others of its ilk are designed

to fly. Wings snapping open like an umbrella lifted by the wind,
neck tucked in, legs sticking out like an oar, the heron soars.
Not entirely lacking in grace, it regains its poise flying solo
circling the sky, cruising with deep wingbeats. When it is ready
to land, it parachutes down to the colony where its tribe resides.

Sparrows

Possessing neither flamboyant color, nor symphonic singing prowess,
the nimble sparrow could easily go unnoticed, were it not for
its overwhelming presence everywhere. It is true that
among its many cousins, variations in hue, shading and texture

are impressive, and songsters can be heard singing
their courtship lyrics. The song sparrow is famed for its springtime
rhapsodies, while the fox sparrow and Lincoln's sparrow carry
the best tunes which, as young sparrows, they have learnt

to mimic by eavesdropping on singing adult males.
For winning looks, at one end sits the white-throated sparrow,
handsome, in a fluffy sort of way. At the other end is the almost
drab, 'old world' creature seen daily out of our windows.

Yet, these clay-colored chirping birds have a certain unassuming
beauty and are readily granted the status of house sparrows
for their industrious spirit. They nest at human eye-level, close
to human dwellings, making a din as they dart and scrimmage

for insects and worms. At the feeder, their table manners
leave a lot to be desired: for every seed they peck,
they scatter ten on the ground, duly swept up by underlings
waiting for crumbs. Their appetite for gossip and chatter is unequalled.

Hummingbird

This next performer, darting into view with an inaudible whir
of transparent wings, is nature's undisputed masterpiece.
Barely four inches long and weighing about as much as a nickel,
the ruby-throated hummingbird is capable of achieving speeds
of up to sixty miles an hour. With wings beating eighty times a second,
it is among the few birds able to fly vertically and in reverse.

It lives on nectar and sweet water using its flawless needle-thin beak
and tongue to probe the hearts of flowers. When preparing
to migrate across the Gulf of Mexico – an incredible
non-stop journey of five hundred miles – the hummingbird
doubles its body mass by fattening on spiders and insects
along with the high-octane nectar to fuel its long, lonely, flight.

Outdone only by the delicate, yet robust, monarch butterfly.
Marathon artists, welcome to my backyard.

Mourning Dove

Less rumpy than the blue-gray pigeon domesticated
over six thousand years ago, employed as a messenger bird
since Caesar's time, is this smaller, slimmer dove with pale brown
plumage, dotted back, and quiet demeanor. It is content to glean
the ground for seeds scattered by noisy sparrows scuffling at the feeder.
It remains above the fray, turning its back on their unseemly frenzy,
not in disdain, but with an almost Buddhist aloofness.
Its soft, slow cooing that resembles oh-woe-oh-woe-oh-woe has earned
for it the name of mourning dove. I hear in its call not an echo
of human sadness, not a wail, but a note that reminds us daily:
I am here, I am here, I am here.

Warbler

If birds had tribal leanings, the most close-knit would be
the clan of warblers. They come in all colors, and go by scores
of distinct family names; they are in perpetual motion and they are born singers.
They sing, even though they are among the most frequent victims
of nest parasitism by their nemesis, the brown-headed cowbirds,
so called because they follow herds of cattle. Not being nest-builders,
the cowbirds lay their eggs in the cradles of other birds
who will often hatch them and raise the young brood as their own.
Not so the warblers, who are smart enough not to be duped.
They either abandon their nests or build them over and over,
creating bizarre multi-layered high-rise nests. You may look
for a note of protest, a trace of complaint in the warbler's song;
but all you hear is sweet-sweet-sweet-summer-sweet, all season long.

In Praise of Father

A Monologue

Dad was born in a Nebraska farmhouse three years before the First Great War, to parents who had migrated from Germany. Grandfather owned about a hundred acres. He raised a few cows and pigs and grew oats, wheat, and corn. In those days they used horses to plough and harvest the fields. If you were a kid growing up on a farm, you worked on the farm and Dad was no exception. He did attend school but only up to the eighth grade. Dad married in 1934, when he was twenty-three. The marriage was arranged by some 'helpful' match-makers.

Five years later, I was born. That was the year the Second Great War began. The Depression had come and gone affecting many of the Nebraska farms. Grandfather, who loved to drink and play cards, spent most of his time in the card hall rather than attending to business at the farm. He eventually lost the farm. Around the same time, Grandma suffered a stroke and was paralyzed for nine years. The image I have of her is that of a gray-haired, heavy-set, loving lady lying in bed who gave me pineapple candy when I went to see her. Because he had a sick mother to look after, Dad was spared from military service during the Second Great War.

After the farm was lost and Grandma passed away, Dad got a job with Standard Oil delivering gas to homes and farms. He left that company after three years and found employment with Nebraska State Fisheries supplying fingerling fish – trout, walleye, catfish – to lakes and ponds. When the fingerling matured, they were caught for sport and food. Our house at the State Fisheries was located on a hill overlooking the ponds. One memory I have is of looking out the window after dark in the winter when the ponds would be lit and frozen, and watching the kids and their parents skating. I attribute my love of the outdoors partly to those magical spaces I grew up in. Today, I go to another lake – not for skating – but ice-fishing. There is nothing to match the silence and solitude I bask in, than being alone on a frozen lake.

After two years of working for the State of Nebraska, Dad decided that his real love was still farming. So, he left that job and farmed in Nebraska for a couple of years before moving to Jefferson Iowa, where he rented a 160-acre farm. Our first piece of farm machinery was a Ford Ferguson tractor which I rode as if I were leading a parade: only, it was a parade of cattle being goaded from the pastures into the barn at milking time. When the tractor was required elsewhere, I rode Old Suzy, my favorite cow, all over the farm.

Dad continued his life on the farm. I helped look after the pigs, and chicken, milked the cows and cleaned their enclosures. We had our own supply of milk, eggs, vegetables, and meat. Dad mainly operated the machinery, while mother canned the peas, carrots, beans, and filled rows of jars with strawberry and gooseberry preserves. Dad had taught me to use a gun to hunt small game. You could say I was a frontiersman in miniature. My trusty dog and I brought home squirrel, rabbit, pheasant, and other birds, and often, that was our dinner. I was not even twelve at the time.

We indulged in small pleasures: a bottle of pop for a nickel and a movie ticket for a dime. I was the only child and I had the best parents anyone could wish for. In my entire childhood, I was never spanked. When she was angry or upset about something, mother would turn to my father to tease him about his height – it was a sore point with him because he was just over five feet tall – and he would pretend to be hurt. But they loved each other ninety percent of the time.

In his early forties, Dad left the farm for health reasons to work at Tesch's gas station. After a couple of years, he left Tesch's and leased his own gas station – Phillips 66. I enjoyed being his assistant at the shop on the weekends and during summer vacations. He was a generous man. He always thought about other people first. He gave his poor customers free supplies, handed out candy by the fistful to kids and helped total strangers. I finished high school, went on to college, got married and around that time, my family and I moved to Michigan. He inculcated the work ethic in me. I am proud to say that in my thirty-eight years of work, I have missed only two days.

At sixty-nine, Dad got prostate cancer and went through the routine chemo-radiation treatment. But in four years, the cancer spread to the bones and he passed away at seventy-two in Arizona, where he used to go to avoid the cold mid-west winters. I was with him then. Three days before he died, he asked me for a cigarette. I lit one for him. As he puffed away peacefully, I noticed the wedding ring. He told me he had never ever taken it off. Mother outlived him by twenty-four years, but that's another story.

Shaving Brush

Let's be honest. I didn't exactly acquire
heirloom status when your father entrusted
me to your youthful custody.
But I stood proud, a sculpted bust
with a red base, yellow belly,
and a full head of prickly hair.
You took to me and I went along
everywhere in your pouch.
We have had some adventures
and mishaps, these fifty years.
From East to West, I helped
brighten your day, even as sometimes
you got carried away in the wrong
direction. Dulled now,
travel-weary, I still do my job
which got a lot easier after you grew
a beard. I am ready for my fate
knowing full well
I will not be handed down
to your unborn son.

Stapler

I was your first,
but you have held on to me
for good. I was borrowed
from the office
and never returned. No one
missed me and I was free
from their rough-handling.
This is home now –
this corner of the desk
where you can reach me
with a stretch of your arm.
I'm a baby croc with open mouth.
A nudge on my nose
and my jaws snap shut.
I stitch corners and paper ends.
I hold words in place,
keep your narrative from breaking
down. We have stuck it out
for forty busy years,
although I am getting a bit rusty
on the edges.
But so are you.

Juicer

They call me old-fashioned –
me, with the pointed head and serrated sides
squatting in a tub where the juice trails down
and collects as if in a moat. Designed for manual
operation, the only external tool required is
a strong wrist with an agile twist. The generation
that followed me has a cup attached below the tray
which turns like a lid. As advances go, this is hardly

breath-taking. Admittedly, there are sleeker,
electronic juicers, but the watchword in this family
is simplicity. So I am fortunate to be enjoying
a long life-span without a dent or a complaint
to mar my reputation. I have to say I have been
sparingly used. In the home where I served, the family
could hardly afford luxuries like using up five oranges

to fill half a glass of juice. Only the sick, when advised
to stay off solid food, were entitled to this preferential
treatment. Today, when cans and bottles supply juice
by the gallon, who has time or the desire for such rituals?
When someone pulls me out from the shadows
in the kitchen cabinet, it is more for the novelty –

as a gesture or overture a loved one makes to do
something special on a slow Sunday morning.

Grater

I am a simple but ingenious device, nine inches tall,
with a broad base and narrow tower topped with
a hand grip. I provide four surfaces armed with notches
for four applications. I am sharp; in fact, I am all steel, designed
to cut down everything to size that lands on my grates – nutmeg,
onions, carrots, cucumber, cheese – anything which can be ground,
sliced, shredded, or diced. After almost constant daily use

for three decades, I am understandably a bit blunted. Not for me
the knife-sharpener. When I lose my edge, it's gone for good.
Although I have been replaced by a newer, sharper, younger
model, I have not been discarded. My mistress has held on
to me for sentimental reasons – I belonged to her mother –
and looks at me from time to time as one would an old
photograph. My more youthful partner stands ladder-like

with two metal plates framed in a hard plastic alloy
whose black smartly offsets the shiny steel in the middle.
Its handgrip looks more like a headrest. When not in use,
it folds like a ladder and lies on its side. You have to take my word
when I say I am not resentful in the least. I have bowed out
gracefully. I have earned my rest and from the glances cast at me,
I have not lost any love either. Finally, I get to sit back and smell the spices.

Tavva

Indian word for a common type of skillet

My tribal links were forged a few millennia ago, but my clan
has dug in to occupy every corner of the earth. I am iron: I am
virtually indestructible. Even when reduced to the lowly state
of scrap, I reincarnate in other shapes and forms.

In my current mould, I am ten inches in diameter, with a gentle
curve from end to end. I have cousins who are larger and come
with wooden handles. The ones used in restaurants and wayside
fast food stalls can be three feet wide and are generally flat-bottomed.

I sit on top of wood fires, flaming coal, gas burners, red-hot electric
coils, waiting for the flip and clang of the flat metallic spatula against
my heated surface that gives raw ingredients new identities. It is then
that I begin to sing. The roadside vendors, performance artists

to the core, flatter me the most, as they draw customers into my
magnetic presence. But that's not me. That street life is for more
seasoned players. I was fashioned for a more domestic space
and in this role, I have spent countless years. I may have lost

my luster but not my grit. I can flip pancakes, omelettes, dosas, crepes,
chappatis, fried fish, and a lot more. I have an impressive repertoire.
You put me to the task and I will prove my metal. I am not Teflon.
A visitor watching my moves burst out: *I want one of those*, she said.

The children in the household say: *Dad, you make the best fried eggs
with crispy underside and edges but the yolk still soft.* I glow with
pride over my contribution. At day's end, I cool down, to be warmed up
again in the morning light. My life is for the long haul. I will go from
hand to hand, age to age. I am meant to outlive mortals. I am iron.

The Book of Recipes

Look at me now: my muscles slack, my sinews coming
undone, my pages limp and falling out, my face decorated with
turmeric stains. You'd be hard-pressed to imagine me in
my prime forty years ago, my mind a blank slate eager to learn
and store the secrets of culinary wizards.

Back when I was unpacked from a fresh consignment of stationery
items sold to school children as notebooks for homework,
my crisp hundred pages with ruled lines were stitched and glued
between hard red-and-yellow covers. What was strictly
an oral tradition of kitchen magic, passed on from mother to daughter

and further advanced under the tutelage of a mother-in-law,
had no need to be recorded. Until the son went West
for further studies and asked to learn a few basic meals. Thus
it was I entered the picture. And the Word became text,
and the text became a blueprint for a garland of dishes.

When the wife came into the family, another script was
added to the three belonging to mother, brother, and sister.
Each of them left footprints in their signature styles that decades later
summon ancestral ties, memories, experiments, and
alterations. Dissolving borders brought home an abundance of tastes

from cooks schooled in the art and rituals of regional cuisines.
I have come to resemble an ancient manuscript, much fussed over:
the guardian of this sacred collection, which can be transcribed to pass on
to a new apprentice. However, in all humility, I sing no odes
to perfection: I am simply an aggregate of names, measures, methods,

the mere recital of which will not bloom into song. A recipe will not of itself
leap from the pages to land into your expectant mouth. It will take all
your sensory prowess to breathe life into these dormant notes. After all,
it is not food alone that satisfies the appetite. It is the devotion
with which you have garnished your offering that satiates the hunger.

Tea Strainer

From the craftsman's hands to the utensil store
to the Hammond home was an uneventful trip. That was
sixty years ago. And although I've moved three times,
having been handed down from mother to son to grandson,
I've been put aside, an item no longer in favor. It was not always so.

Although the teabag had been invented by a canny trader
in a far country, the Hammonds, like the rest of
the British population, were not about to abandon
their sacred tea rituals which entailed steeping loose tea
leaves in hot water, thus making the strainer a necessary

accomplice in that act. I was fussed over, my chrome-silver face
given a scrub and polish to keep me in sterling condition.
From my perch, I have seen and heard it all during my tenure:
gossip, tears, and laughter; choices wise and foolish, the remixing
of the changing colors of unreliable memories. With the closing

of that era, my active life ended. Look at me now – showing no signs
of age, I still wear the proud glint of my youth. You could say I've led
a charmed life. Of no practical use now, I sit on a china base
among other oddities on a shelf in a glass case, simply looking
ornamental, an object of wonder for the new set of tea-drinkers.

The Pipe

for my good friend, Ron

From the mines of Turkey to the vast plains of Iowa
is a long trail. That is how I came to be transformed
from the raw clay of my origin to the hard meerschaum
of my birth as a pipe. I was one among many on show,
striking a pose on the velvet and satin-lined case, my stem
and bowl designed in the style made famous by Sherlock Holmes.

My purpose in life was clear: to provide pleasure and peace, and,
in Sherlock's case, to help his brain connect the dots.
But who would have thought, a father giving his son a pipe
as a graduation gift? Which is how I landed in this remote
farmhouse in the hands of a lad just out of college.
Ron was thrilled – I cost quite a bundle in those days, in the 60s –

at his father's extravagance, seeing that he was a man of
modest means. I gave my lad a certain elegance, a glow of
assurance every time he inhaled, whether at his study table
or at social events; in the rocking chair out on the porch in
the starry night, or ice-fishing on the hard surface of a frozen lake.
I was his steady companion, though not the only one.

Ron loved tobacco and he smoked cigarettes as well. You can guess
what's coming next. His lungs took it well, but what undid him
was a heart attack at sixty-two. He had no choice but to give up
smoking. But he was not letting me go. I am his father's love
made visible. So I wait in my container whose outer edges have been
chewed by a mouse, leaving scars. The inside is warm though

and cosy, not unlike a violin case which senses the vibrations of
the instrument's strings long after the concert is over.

The Masseuse

A Monologue

My family tree looks much like that of other migrants who set out for the New World. My European origins go back to Sicily from where my maternal grandmother came as an orphan to be adopted by a family in Cleveland. She ended by marrying a son of that family. My father's background is a mix of German, Swiss, and French. He was born and raised in Michigan. He sold reconditioned typewriters, then switched to computers and joined my brother in founding their own software company. Mom was a school teacher all her life. Their marriage lasted seven years

during which time my brother and I were born. After my parents parted, we lived with our Mom during the week and weekends with my father. It was special being with him; we had so much fun. When I was nine, Mom was diagnosed with breast cancer. She was only thirty-seven. She was in remission a year later and remained that way for four years. She spent the next seven years trying alternative treatments. She died at forty-nine, when I had turned twenty-one.

When he remarried, my father and my stepmom had two kids of their own. With the arrival of my stepmother began a turbulent phase in our lives. She was truly the fairytale 'evil stepmom' who thrived on drama and chaos. Her rages were nasty and frequent. She did not talk: she yelled, screamed, threw things and broke them. To her credit it should be noted that she berated all the kids, including her own. While we all spent Christmas Eve together, Christmas Day was reserved only for her family. We were not welcome on vacations either. The one time she displayed some compassion was looking after mother when she was sick. Whenever she left town to visit her family in Chicago, the grey cloud hanging over the house dissolved and we cherished those days without her.

Why did Dad stay with her? He did not want to lose the kids or leave them in her care. What did Dad see in her in the first place? Kids never ask these questions and if they do, they never get proper answers. Life in school was another type of hell. I was the 'fat' girl. And my brother, in typical brotherly fashion, called me stupid. I became shy and lacked any kind of self-confidence. After a trip to Broadway one summer, my dream was to be a chorus girl. Another time, after a visit to San Diego and the ocean, I thought I wanted to be a marine biologist. I went to college directly after high school, but only for a semester. I really didn't want to be there since I had no clear idea what I wanted to study. I had lived in a fantasy world. As a young girl, my book of dreams was the Sear's catalogue. A friend and I would mark all the fancy things we wanted in the catalogue, but were dismayed that they cost thousands of dollars. These things we could acquire only by marrying a man of means. He would also be our ticket to freedom, away from family constraints: every girl's naïve hope.

So at twenty-one, I found a man, a mechanical engineer, to marry me and we moved out to Colorado and later to Arizona where we built a sustainable solar-powered house. We were out on an adventure, defying and disowning our middle class upbringing. Ironically, first I was a stay-at-home wife, then stay-at-home mother. I went to community college for two years. When I got a 4.0 GPA, I realized I was smart and I loved learning. I was not 'stupid' after all. It took many years and detours to make that discovery. It was then that I went to Massage Therapy School. I was thirty-four and still a stay-at-home mom. But not for long.

After two sons were born four years apart, we decided it was time to move back to Michigan to be near the rest of the family. We bought a farmhouse. But ahead lay another turn. Differences began to unravel our marriage, ultimately resulting in divorce. I had married for the wrong reasons and those reasons had landed me here. It was as simple as that. After my parents had separated, they had continued to be friends. Learning that lesson enabled my husband and I to part on cordial terms.

While I was able to make a living to support myself and the boys, I still believed I was incomplete without a man. It took a couple of relationships for me to see that I was going round the same loop, reliving the old patterns. I stepped back from these involvements and found that I was no longer afraid to be alone. I realized that in order to feel secure, I had to find my own worth within myself. The peace I had found in the Arizona desert and the serenity I experienced in nature – I had to draw this inward to infuse every fiber of my being. Of vital importance to me is the idea of healing. All through life, we accumulate hurts and scars and we need to find ways to cleanse and restore our primal selves to bring into harmony our body and mind, our heart and spirit. What helped me along were the values my parents had instilled in me: my mother was a spirited woman unafraid to try anything; my father taught me to keep going, to finish what I started. When I look back on how things have stacked up and examine each element, what I want to pass on to my sons is to make sure they don't repeat the mistakes I made. They will face their own challenges as they follow their individual pathways in life. People waste time and energy nurturing grievances and raking up old familial grouses. They poison not only personal relationships, but ignite major generational feuds which lead to destructive societal consequences. The world needs less of this. And we must begin with ourselves.

Anatomy of a Fig

The fruit with the longest history on earth, the fig
is also believed to be the first farmed fruit.

In Eden, the fig leaf failed its mission – the fruit hung
immodestly from the tree, tender as a testicle. Its skin

shading goes from yellow and brown to resplendent purple.
In the market, the figs sit on their ample rumps

neatly arrayed in a basket. Pick one by its nubby stem
and gently sink your teeth into its glistening wet, lush red

yellow-dotted interior. No seed or nut to bar your way –
just a mouthful of oozing, melting, flesh to sweeten your life.

Even so, like most other fruit, the fig survives in an altered state
in a new incarnation. Drying in the sun, the fig

folds into itself, curling its stem down
to its flat belly, hoarding its honey for a second act.

In Praise of Persimmons

Celebrated in Chinese and Japanese art, the persimmon
grows in clumps on a canopy of branches. It is routinely

pecked by parrots, nibbled by fat ants, filched
by monkeys. Its smooth, orange skin distinguishes it

from its lookalike, the tomato. But what sets it apart
is the dry, curly, brittle, four-leaf top it wears for headcover.

The persimmon is for those who are in no hurry to attack
the fruit. Like a hard kiwi, eat it too soon

when it is not ripe, and your mouth will protest. With a hard
persimmon, the inside of your mouth will turn chalky.

You have to wait until the fruit decides it is ready.
Then its astringency will have faded, and it will reward

your patience by yielding its soft, velvety flesh
with a sweetness matched only by your memory of mangoes.

Pomegranate

Lift, to feel the weight of this globed fruit in your palm.
Beneath the smooth, red, exterior complexion is a thick
hide wound tight around itself. What it reveals,
as you quarter the fruit and the four sections rock open
to your astonished gaze, is a glitter of stars studded
like rubies. They bleed as you bend back each slice

to free the seeds from the honeycomb of white membrane.
There is an art to doing this and patience counts, or the seeds
will spring out and red-spot everything within close range.
Delivered of its precious cargo, the womb of a shell
lies empty, de-toothed. The pomegranate is peculiar in that
the fruit *is* the seed: around each seed is a sliver

of crunchy flesh. Eat it by the spoonful and feel how
the sweet, cool, juice is released in your mouth, and without
any fuss the seeds, whether chewed or not, travel down
your gullet. There are other ways too of enjoying this fruit.
Garnish your salads with it, add it to yogurt, and if you can stand
the sweet, bitter edge, drink a glass of this virtuous brew.

The Measure of a Mango

If its fragrance does not instantly captivate you,
its nubile shape will make you want to caress it.

For those cultivating mangoes in orchards or backyards
the springtime appearance of mango blossoms is a sight

heralding a summer harvest. Plentiful every season, mangoes flood
the market: vendors peddle cartloads of small hillocks

of fruit, and bazaar stalls display them in cardboard cases.
Door-to-door sellers, sweating in the sun, carry baskets

that stack four storeys of mangoes layered in hay. Raw mangoes
can be laid on a blanket under the bed to ripen.

For heft and smooth texture, taste and aroma, the Alphonso
by common consent, has no equal. Among the dozens of breeds,

each with its own appeal and region of origin, there is even
a mango that when cut open, releases a fly from the nut.

There are fibrous mangoes best suited for sucking: you press and
roll them around in your palm, take the stub off the top, and

in a prolonged kiss, draw the juice out with your lips.
The mango is nothing if not versatile. It can be mixed in yogurt *lassi,*

milkshakes, ice cream, fruit salad, or served as pulp with *puris, roti,*
or rice. Raw mango is a treat in itself, stolen from a wayside tree,

sliced and sprinkled with salt and chili powder for a school girl's
snack, or diced and added to *bhel.* It handily answers the cravings

of pregnant women for sour-tart. It can be juiced up for
a refreshing, ice-cold, summer drink. Spicy raw mango pickle

and shredded mango *chhunda* are national table favorites.
How to handle a ripe mango should you encounter one?

It does not pay to be dainty with the mango. The closer
your hands get to the bare rump of the mango

the greater the satisfaction of devouring it. When you slice it,
you may keep the skin intact, cut sideways around the central nut,

then from each slice, bite off chunks of flesh with your teeth. The nut
with ridges of fruit still around it, offers the ultimate pleasure

of nibbling, juice dripping down your fingers. A long-time friend,
a Sister of Mercy, a visitor to Jamaica, and a confirmed addict of mangoes

offers this instruction: strip your clothes off, get into a tub, and
gorge on a plateful of peeled mangoes with your bare hands.

Excess, not moderation, is the true measure of mangoes.

Regarding the Orange

When the atmosphere is so thick with the sweet tangy scent
that your body has to slice the air to wade through –
that is how a citrus grove blossoms out. When you enter
a house, you can tell oranges are in the room before you notice
someone peeling an orange at the far end of the table. And, as if
an entire orchard has been packed into the single fruit
you've just eaten, your orange-fresh breath draws your mate
to seek your mouth for an urgent, unforgettable kiss.

It is thought to be the most widely-grown fruit tree
in the world. Ever since the Chinese first cultivated it
four thousand five hundred years ago, travelers carried
seeds and saplings to plant them in their native soil to create
dozens and dozens of hybrid blends whose names ring
like the chimes of bells – clementines, tangerines, tangelos,
mandarin, malta, navel, hamlin, valencia, blood, and more.
In South Asia, the orange is clearly differentiated from

the sweet lemon, called *mosambi*. The orange contains
neatly separable slices that come delicately wrapped as if
in tissue. On the other hand, the sweet lemon's thicker rind,
as opposed to the orange's loose-fitting tunic, has to be pared
with a knife. Its robust interior is a compact ball of flesh
to be cut into pieces. In markets elsewhere, most growers
call *this* an orange. When juiced, there is a subtle but clear
difference in taste between the two. The orange has a touch

of tart from its higher acidic level. The *mosambi* tends to be
sweeter but paler, without the tang. The Nagpur orange variety,
strangely unrecorded in orange lore outside Asia, is the most
prized in the subcontinent and can be quickly stripped down
past the white threads and skin membranes to the shiny flesh.
Marmalade originated centuries ago in Greco-Roman times
but, according to popular belief, was invented by the Scots.
In the 18th century, a Spanish ship took refuge from a raging storm

in the harbor town of Dundee. Its cargo of oranges was purchased
by a local grocer and it was his wife, Mrs. Keillor, who saw the potential
of these overripe oranges. She boiled them – with the pips and rinds –
added sugar, and bottled the preserves to sell them as marmalade.
Now, Seville oranges with slivered or rough-cut peels make the best
marmalade, with a high edge of bitter. No matter what shape or size
oranges come in or what names they go by, no matter if their sweet
syllables are tinged by sour notes; their primary attribute, their
redolent fragrance, has carried them far and wide. Orange halves, like the sun
rising or setting, wash our world in the mist of their warm, mellow light.

Guava

It comes in three glistening shades – yellow, maroon, or green.
Pear-shaped or rounded, it has a heady fragrance that can fill
a room. Its interior can be white or pink. Its center is sprinkled
with seeds as hard as tiny pellets but which are meant
to be eaten. Like raw mango, the un-ripened guava

in its hard state makes an agreeable snack when chewed
with a dash of salt and chili powder. When soft, it can be cut
into quarters or bitten into like an apple. Cooked,
sweetened, and served with custard, it makes for an utterly
ravishing dessert. As with fig preserves, only the most

discerning are drawn to the taste of guava jam,
and the drink from guava extract is like a rush, awakening
all the senses. But beyond spreading summery
delights, the guava serves an even higher purpose:
the fruit is a favorite of birds and animals too.

Chikoo

Going by appearance alone, its dour, unwashed look
will more than likely make you doubt its table-worthiness.
Color, shape, size: all accentuate its lack of personality.
Round or oval, it is no bigger than a golf ball.
Its dull brown skin, which can be leathery or paper-thin,
provides neither glow nor glamour. It has no scent to speak of.

That said, let's sample one. Leave the rough-skinned aside,
for its grainy flesh, like that of a grainy pear, is not the best
it can offer. Peel the one with the smooth complexion
and slice down the middle into four equal parts. As it opens
like a flower, a couple of shiny black almond-shaped
seeds will slide out. Be sure to remove the thin white

center line off the top, which can be slightly bitter.
What you have now is brownish-pink flesh which is soft
and glossy, with an exceptionally sweet, malty flavor.
Chew slowly to spread the sweetness around in
your mouth. Having taken its time, to make you want
more, the chikoo has finally insinuated its peculiar charm.

A Paean to the Papaya

There were two kinds of papaya trees in the backyard
of my childhood: the ones that bore a spray of flowers
and others that were stacked with green fruit. It was my first
lesson in horticulture: papaya trees, my mother would say,
come in two genders – neuter and female.

Slice open a ripe papaya from stem to stern and you'll find
a boatload of black, peppery pellets. Scrape these out
and take in the colors of this fruit, which may range
from yellow to orange to blushing pink. Then cut out the thick
peel, cube the flesh, and feel its sweetness melt in your mouth.

Raw papaya was among the variety of pickles made
by the women in the family. Diced papaya was combined with
sliced carrot, fresh ginger and turmeric, seasoned with
mustard and soaked in vinegar, then bottled for daily use.
It was a strong, sour, salty, crunchy blend that puckered
my mouth, for which I developed a taste only later in life.

Going Bananas: A Discourse

Between its ideal freshness and its prime, to its rapid decline,
lies the short history of the banana's brief lifespan.

Being an all year round fruit, it found its way into our home
every day. As the most affordable to people of limited means,

it provided us with the comfort of knowing even *we* could enjoy
the luxury of fruit three times a day. Because its skin spotted fast

and it rotted quickly, it was bought daily from the bazaar, or from
the vendor with the head-basket who did his daily rounds.

But an overripe banana is never to be wasted. For a sweet dish
you cut up round pieces, add a dollop of ghee, a dash of sugar,

and ground cardamom, and cook it for two minutes. Or substitute
jaggery for sugar. Mashed or sliced pieces, dipped in batter

and shallow-fried, make incredible banana fritters.
Lacking ovens or blenders, we could not bake banana bread

or whip up smoothies. In south India, the plantain
leaf is recycled as a disposable dinner plate. Cultivated for mass

production in miles of plantations, banana trees also thrive
in back alley gardens fed by gutter water. The fruit comes in a medley of

sizes, shapes, colors, textures, and tastes. Some are tinier than fingers,
others as long and large as cucumbers. They grow in concentric

circles around a thick trunk which has the appearance of an inverted
conical tree. Lifting one of these branches is a muscular feat.

Some bananas are cooked in their raw stage but most others
need to be matured for the market. This curvy, humble fruit can

hold its head high for its simplicity, its sweet nature, its character
traits, and its worldwide domination. In the native grounds where

it flourished, the state's regimes were branded, quite undeservedly,
as Banana Republics. Inevitably, the Empire, having lost its stride

and its nerve as well, was headed for a fall: triggering laughter,
the banana's slippery peel does make clowns of us all.

The Curious Case of the Custard Apple

If ever a fruit was misnamed, this one had the misfortune of getting
virtually defaced. The British had a hand in writing the anglicized

versions of not only fruits and vegetables, but also of larger entities
such as cities, rivers, mountains, and streets. Not to mention

the changing of personal names which saved them the bother
of training their tongues around those slippery syllables.

The fruit's native name is sitaphal, or Sita's favored fruit,
for which there is a male counterpart ramphal, or fruit

beloved by Rama, which, even if it makes no linguistic point, confers
on it mythological status. Bound in a green-brown jacket

resembling bubble wrap, sitaphal has the hard look of a grenade,
only rounder. When ripe, it has to be handled with care

or the fruit will easily smash. If the skin is shading into black
the fruit is close to hitting its expiry date. When ready to eat

the fruit opens in half in your hand so, holding it like a saucer,
you can dip your lips into it for morsels of sweet, milky, flesh,

while deftly spitting out the shiny black seeds.
That is all there is to it. Except, that the fruit also ranks high

as a frozen treat: as a flavor, sitaphal ice cream, available only
in season, vies with mango, pistachio, and saffron. No doubt

the British palate was tickled when the fruit struck its custardy chords.
So we'll consider this misnomer as a tribute to the sitaphal.

Cracking a Coconut

They're everywhere, fringing the shorelines or growing in thick groves
in the interiors of tropical lands. The wind rustles the tree tops
and the fronds sway sensuously, as if warming up for a dance.
Not being subject to the seasons, the trees produce an abundant

cycle of crops. The fresh green fruit which descends from the tree
that is sold for coconut water, is a different proposition
to the ball of hard nut with three eyes stocked in the store
which you can easily dismantle in your kitchen.

The baby coconut's white fiber can be shaved off at the bottom end
with a sharp paring knife. Then a lid is carved to make a hole
out of which you can drink the cool, sweet, nectar. The tender flesh
of the baby coconut – a delicacy to die for – you can scoop out like cream.

What I know about splitting a coconut, I learnt as a boy, watching
an expert the family hired to harvest the crop from the seven trees
in our yard. The first requisite – you must approach a coconut as if
you are about to knock heads with a tough opponent. It will offer

resistance, but if you make the right moves, it will yield.
When the coconut has matured, the fiber is dry and stringy
and can be taken apart by a deftly-handled sickle. The bone-like nut
can either be cracked neatly in half around the middle, or

if you lack finesse, smashed with a hammer into uneven pieces.
The dazzling hard flesh, pried loose with a knife, makes a wholesome
snack by itself, or sweetened with dates or jaggery, a form of unrefined
lump sugar. The many uses of coconut in soups, chutneys, curries,

sweets, desserts, oils, cosmetics, is legendary. But that is only
half the story. The coconut shell can be burnt to produce
tooth powder. The fiber is used to make rope, coir mats, and stuffing
for furniture. The trunk offers strong timber for water-craft

and the large palm leaves provide light roof covering for huts.
Seeming to live forever, the coconut tree stands tall, even in its afterlife.

Pineapple

Although clad in armor, with eyes all over its body looking
as if it is keeping watch, it lowers its gaze when

you meet it. It is a pity that in order to reach its fleshy
interior, you have to be so rough with this peaceful fruit:

lop off its crown of thorns, slice the bottom flat, then
gouge its eyes out as you proceed to take off its armor.

Discard the hard cylindrical core if you prefer, quarter it
or halve it length-wise, cut circles, or cubes, or sticks

or shred it, depending on where it is going – salad,
shake, sherbet, cake, custard. The golden ones are

the sweetest. On a hot day, you can count on its juice
to quench your thirst and calm your insides like any citrus

fruit does. Strangely, its acidity can tame a greasy meal.
Its fragrance alone can make some people happy.

Lychee

On the outside, a dull rust-red rind
rough to the touch, though not the kind
to make it a burr. Easy enough to be
nipped and peeled with a pen-knife
or fingernails. If you are quick enough

you can suck the sweet juice before it spills out.
What you now have is a dull-white translucent
ball of flesh wrapped around a hard, shiny
brown seed. Pop this into your mouth to do
what your tongue and teeth are designed

to do to any pitted fruit – rend apart the flesh
from the seed. Remember, the lychee has been
cultivated for four thousand years. As you roll it
around in your mouth, close your eyes in reverence,
and think of it as manna from China.

Tea-time Tales

A Chinese sage leaves a bowl of hot water unattended
and the wind blows some leaves into it. He decides to sip
the yellow-green liquid and, to his surprise, finds the taste
agreeable and his mood elevated. Thus came about the discovery
of the tea plant in the tenth century BC. Legend pushed it
back another seventeen centuries to credit Shennong
with the invention. Initially, tea was used for medicinal
purposes and also as a stimulant that 'makes one think better.'

The tea plant was given a sonorous botanical name:
camellia sinensis. Its place of origin lies somewhere on the border
where northern Myanmar meets Southwest China. Before long
it spread to surrounding regions and distant lands. After water,
tea is the most widely consumed brew, with hundreds of varieties
of tea leaves and methods of preparation, and additives that make
for distinctive tea cultures even within the confines of a single
country. Plantations in Darjeeling, Assam, Nilgiris, and Sri Lanka

cultivate aromas unique to their soils. Like black pepper or cinnamon
over which European traders fought fierce sea battles, this humble leaf
made fortunes for tea smugglers. At the far end of the Empire, it hosted
the Boston Tea Party. Weak tea served with treats in delicate porcelain
is the mark of high tea rituals. Spiked with masala, sweet, steamy, milky chai
ladled out in chipped cups is sold at roadside tea-stalls. For weary travelers
at railway stations, tea is dispensed in disposable earthenware mugs.
There are no protocols for tea. The cup which soothes as it stimulates,

inaugurates the day. It provides a mid-morning break and follows
the afternoon siesta. It welcomes a guest, lubricates conversation.
Back-slapping friends split a cup into halves in a saucer, often accompanied
by bun-maska, in Irani restaurants. It is the cup over which confidences
are shared, rumors are spread, and business deals are sealed.
It is the central player in the drama of match-making: a novice girl of
tender age, balancing a tray of tea cups, walks awkwardly into
the drawing room bazaar, gaze lowered, to be scrutinized by strangers.

Discomfort Foods

The general rule to follow is to eat three heavy meals a day
rich in carbs, fat, and sugar. Start with a farmer's breakfast.
Two eggs at the very least are a must. Disregard the claims
and counter-claims of experts on this subject. Go for
plenty of bread, buns, croissants slathered with butter and jam.
Ham, bacon, sausage can be rotated through the week
and hash browns are optional. Pour a full jar of syrup on
your stack of pancakes. The stack is important to prove that

you are a real man. On this issue, trust the ads imprinted
on your brain. Coffee or tea is necessary to wash it all down.
There are no limits on refills. Go back for orange juice if
you have overlooked that item. Your day-long burping only
goes to show that you have begun your day successfully
with a properly discomforting breakfast. This is a good start.

If you don't feel the pangs of hunger at lunch time, go ahead
and have a hearty lunch. A buffet is ideal, but burgers and fries
will serve just as well. After all, you have to keep company with
your office buddies. When you get home from your all-day-long
sitting job, you will need to flop down in front of the TV
for a beer or two. That is, if you haven't already stopped at
the bar on the way back. Then you are ready for what awaits you:

that sumptuous dinner which you will attack with gusto. One more
step remains. To get the maximum benefit out of your flawlessly
designed and executed eating itinerary so that you may attain
the highest level of discomfort, it is essential that you go
to bed on a full stomach. That is the proper ending to a hard day.
After all, what good is life if not lived in the moment?

Body Primal

Body sprung from a seedling.
A misshapen, spongy mess feeding
on ancient slime, fish-tailing past
oceans, continents, to scream its cry
of arrival. The body in miniature –
bathed, nursed, swaddled in

fragrant baby skin. Body learning
the language of discovery, falling in love
with mirrors. Thrilled by the eloquence
of its limbs, body growing wings,
leaping, dancing, taking off.
The body lost in search of itself.

The Body in Question

Glorified at the hands
of artists, feasted upon by poets,
its praises sung by music-makers.
Dissected by physicians,
its machinery exposed in
anatomy textbooks.

In repose, its beauty drunk
in stillness. Desire awakened
in languor, the flesh animated,
transported in slow motion
to bliss. From the bud of infancy
to maternal bloom. Pushing its limits

to perform daring feats. Body painted,
perfumed, jeweled, and tattooed.
Wet skin in wet clothes. The veiled body
kept in the dark. Body married
to Christ. Paraded on stage, dressed up
or stripped down. Sold and humbled

into submission. Bodies in whose soil
is grown cotton, cane, corn, and tobacco
to make nations rich. Those bodies still
slogging on, impoverished. Bodies from
which coal is mined and gold is extracted.
Body rewarded, eroding with disease.

Migrating bodies washed ashore.
The body detached, its primal urges
mastered by yogis; its potential sunk
in self-indulgence. Body behind bars.
In solitary. Body effaced in suicide. Body
stopping bullets, blown to cinders by bombs.

In genocide, counted in numbers.
Body in pain, suffering blows, coming
to understand its frailty. Eventually
betrayed by its own failure, losing muscle,
bone, attaining stasis, shutting down.
The body home at last, laid out cold.

Body Carnal

Utter the word
and it triggers
a reproach, an internal
whiplash. The sheer
audacity of it –
to burn for what is
out of bounds,
not yours to have.

Drive this unruly lust out
of your mind.
Let it drain
out of your toes and
fingertips.
If the impulse rears
its head again,
just
strangle
it.

Message

Out here, the cold wind
                    rules
from September to May
                    whistling
right through the tunnel
                    of my ears, making
my toes curl.

I stretch my hand looking
                    for yours
but you have been reported
                    missing.

Out there
            when you feel a chill go
                    up your spine,

listen to what the wind
                    is saying
                            as it rattles
your window-panes.

The Street Walks

The street walks hand in hand
with you.
The subway
picks you up
for a ride.
Bridges bounce you
on their laps.
Traffic lights wink
as you pass.
The park spreads
its arms
to receive you.
The sidewalk café
waits
with an empty table
where you will sit
to compose
a poem
that will make
something
out of nothing.

The Divide

If touch is elemental, animal –
what attaches a mother
to her newborn,
chicks nestling in the underbelly,
a brood of lion cubs tumbling
over each other,
what passes in silence between
man and horse,
a brush of wings,
walruses lounging, hide sticking
to thick hide,
furry creatures rubbing
against tree bark
to calm an itch,
wild and tame seeking kinship
in touch –
then this divide, my sweet,
that feeds my grief
will have to be crossed.

Letter

This is just to say
that I am dismantling the fantasy
I had built with such ease,
in such a hurry, with little thought
but with such precision –
it began to have a life of its own
whose summons I could answer at will.

I am taking back my words,
tearing up the script that would have been
our story. We are miles apart,
so I will not be devising schemes
for accidental run-ins. When the mist
has cleared, I will think of this as a squall
that drenched us and passed on.

Lightning Source UK Ltd.
Milton Keynes UK
UKOW01f0035110616

276029UK00003B/59/P